Keep me clean!

Please don't handle me with soiled hands.

AUTHOR'S NOTE

New York City's Grand Central Terminal is experiencing a renaissance. When it was saved from the threat of destruction in the 1970s, it underwent a major restoration to return the building to its original, glorious state. Now it sparkles like a jewel, to be admired by tens of thousands of daily commuters.

Unfortunately, I am not one of those lucky commuters. My train stops at Pennsylvania Station. I was only four years old when the original Penn Station was destroyed, and I regret that I never had a chance to visit this marvelous building.

But I was given the chance to experience old Penn Station in a different way. In 2003, when I was a student in the master's program at Syracuse University, I decided the subject of my thesis would be the original Pennsylvania Station. This, I felt, was a wonderful opportunity to create art for a new picture book about the birth, life, and death of a much loved building. And so I began my journey in search of old Penn Station—a journey to bring it back to life.

I would like to dedicate this book to Murray Tinkelman
and the late David Passalacqua.

Old Penn Station

WILLIAM LOW

HENRY HOLT AND COMPANY
NEW YORK

In the 1890s, the Pennsylvania Railroad Company was one of the most powerful businesses in the United States. It had the biggest steam locomotives and its tracks reached every major city from Boston to Chicago.

Every major city but one—New York.
That's because the heart of New York City
is an island called Manhattan. Since the
Pennsylvania Railroad Company had no
access to bridges or tunnels
into Manhattan, its
trains could not cross
the Hudson River.
When the conductor
called out, "Last stop!
All passengers off for
New York!" everyone
was still in New Jersey.

Passengers who wanted to go to
New York City had to take the ferry.

But the mighty Pennsylvania Railroad Company was determined to have its trains cross the Hudson River into Manhattan, and wanted to do it with style.

So the company hired the architectural firm of McKim, Mead & White to design a "palace" on West Thirty-second Street for the new electric trains, which were fast replacing the older, steam-driven locomotives.

Hundreds of men were put to work. Tunnel workers called sandhogs burrowed slowly under the Hudson River. A half-million cubic feet of pink granite were cut from the quarries of Milford, Massachusetts. Stonemasons carved these blocks into clocks, maidens, and majestic eagles, designed by the famous sculptor Adolph Alexander Weinman.

The station was completed in 1910. Trains going to Manhattan came through New Jersey and continued down the new tunnels under the river until they reached their final destination.

"Last stop, Pennsylvania Station," the conductor would call out. "Welcome to New York City!"

From the platform, passengers could see the sky. The station's concourse looked like a magical spider-web of metal and glass.

Penn Station workers were proud of their new building, and they worked hard to keep everything clean, shiny, and working in tip-top shape.

Passengers who were lost or needed assistance with their bags asked a friendly Penn Station porter for help.

Passengers who needed a haircut,
shave, or a spit-and-polish shoeshine
went to the first-class barbershop by
the station concourse.

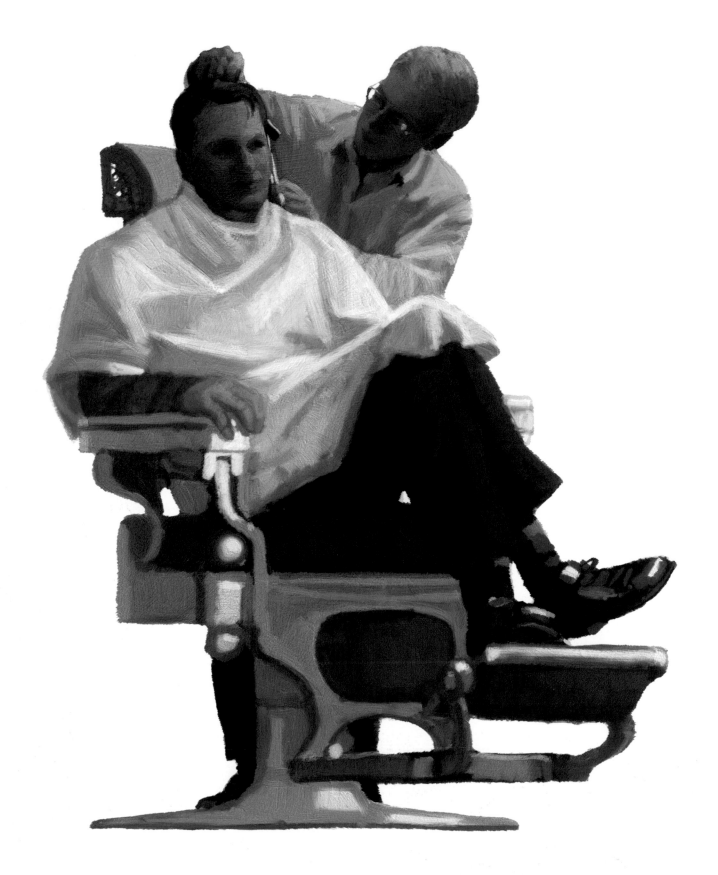

Passengers who were hungry could have dinner
at the fabulous Savarin Restaurant.

Passengers who were tired could sit in the marvelous waiting room. Sunlight streamed through the windows, filling the room with dappled light. For many, it was a magical experience.

The wonderful station was built to move people.
At the end of World War II, hundreds of thousands of
soldiers and officers crowded the concourse to return
home to their families.

When the war ended, Americans wanted new lives. They wanted to marry, start families, and buy new cars and houses in the suburbs. In the 1950s, highways were built to connect these houses to the city, and many people began to see trains as old-fashioned. The leaders of the Pennsylvania Railroad Company couldn't imagine how trains would fit into this new world. They tried to modernize the station and their trains, but nothing worked. As a result, the great Penn Station struggled to survive.

The Pennsylvania Railroad Company was losing money, so its leaders came up with a plan. They decided to make Penn Station smaller and move it underground. They would then build a brand-new sports stadium and a modern office tower on top.

But before this could be done, the
magnificent building had to be torn down.

As Penn Station was destroyed, the shell of Madison Square Garden and the new Penn Plaza was built. Jackhammers rattled. Bulldozers pushed. Cranes lifted new beams up and carried old beams down. The station remained open, despite the noise and dirt. Many passengers had to run to their trains to escape the turmoil.

During the demolition, nothing was spared, not even the statues. Sledgehammers werc used to dismantle the clocks and the sculptures of the maidens. A few people looked up when the cranes came for the eagles. But no one could stop the destruction.

A few of the statues were saved and
found new homes in museums and other
places around the country. But most of
the debris was shipped across the river
and dumped into the marshes of the
New Jersey Meadowlands.

In 1966, the bulldozers, dump trucks, and cranes left West Thirty-second Street. The palace was gone forever. New Yorkers did not realize what they had until it was taken away.

After the destruction of Penn Station, many people were angry. Some became outraged enough to start the New York City Landmarks Preservation Commission, which promised to save other beautiful old buildings from the wrecking ball and to preserve the charm of the city.

This commission kept its promise when it saved Grand Central Terminal and many other historic buildings from the same fate that had befallen Penn Station.

The great Pennsylvania Railroad Station was much more than a train station. It was designed to be a monument to rail travel—its beauty and grandeur were gifts to the city.

Today, the memory of Penn Station's destruction still lingers, and it has become a powerful symbol, a reminder that buildings are not just concrete and steel. They are the heart and soul of all great cities.

BIBLIOGRAPHY AND SUGGESTED READING

Abbott, Berenice. *New York in the Thirties*. New York: Dover Publications, 1973.

Ballon, Hillary. *New York's Pennsylvania Stations*. New York: W. W. Norton & Company, 2002.

Diehl, Lorraine B. *The Late, Great Pennsylvania Station*. New York: Four Walls Eight Windows, 1996.

Hine, Lewis W. *Men at Work*. New York: Dover Publications, 1977.

Moore, Barbara, ed. *The Destruction of Penn Station*. New York: Distributed Art Publishers, 2000.

Parissien, Steven. *Station to Station*. London: Phaidon Press, 1997.

Silver, Nathan. *Lost New York*. New York: Houghton Mifflin Company, 1967.

White, Samuel G., and Elizabeth White. *McKim, Mead & White: The Masterworks*. New York: Rizzoli International Publications, 2003.

Henry Holt and Company, LLC, *Publishers since 1866*,
175 Fifth Avenue, New York, New York 10010 [www.henryholtchildrensbooks.com]

Henry Holt® is a registered trademark of Henry Holt and Company, LLC.
Copyright © 2007 by William Low. All rights reserved. Distributed in Canada by H. B. Fenn and Company Ltd.

Library of Congress Cataloging-in-Publication Data
Low, William. Old Penn Station / William Low.—1st ed.   p.   cm.
ISBN-13: 978-0-8050-7925-8 / ISBN-10: 0-8050-7925-4
1. Pennsylvania Station (New York, N.Y.) 2. New York (N.Y.)—Buildings, structures, etc. 3. Historic buildings—
New York (State)—New York. I. Title. TF302.N7L69 2007   385.3'14097471—dc22   2006015359

First Edition—2007 / Designed by Patrick Collins
Printed in China on acid-free paper. ∞

10 9 8 7 6 5 4 3 2 1